SPILL
YOUR
GUTS!

SPILL
THE ULTIMATE
YOUR
CONVERSATION GAME
GUTS!

BOB BASSO

**Andrews McMeel
Publishing**

Kansas City

SPILL YOUR GUTS!
THE ULTIMATE CONVERSATION GAME

ISBN: 0-7407-3313-3

Library of Congress Catalog Control Number:
2002111556

03 04 05 06 07 BID 10 9 8 7 6 5 4 3 2 1

CONTENTS

INTRODUCTION

Spill Your Guts! is a dangerous game. The questions are deeply personal, provocative, and sometimes naughty, with no room to hide. You don't have time to think; you must be impulsive and say the first thing that pops into your mind, and that usually comes straight from your gut. The truth may set you free, but it can also be shocking, funny, confusing, and sad.

If that's too hot to handle for you and your partner, abandon the rules and just make it a conversation game with no time limit; otherwise, let it rip and let the truth chips fall where they may.

Rules:

1. One person reads. The other person responds by filling in the blank in three seconds or less.

2. The reader indicates the time by holding up three fingers and pulling one down every second.
3. If the respondent answers within three seconds, move to the next question.
4. If the respondent doesn't answer within three seconds, note the number of the question and come back to it later for discussion.
5. Decide in advance how many statements the reader is going to read before you reverse roles.

If there are more than two players:

6. Allow each player to take his/her turn as a respondent to each set of questions.
7. All other rules apply.

GETTING STARTED ZONE

IMMEDIATE REALITY CHECK

Each player must answer these questions before starting.
This is a pregame warm-up to get you in the mood.
There is no time limit in this section only.

My full name is _____, but if I could choose
any name it would be _____
_____.

If I'm going to lie about anything personal it would
probably be about _____
_____.

The one word that describes where I am right now in my
life is _____.

What I like about where I am right now is _____
_____.

What I don't like is _____
_____.

If I weren't doing what I am doing right now to earn a
living, I would be _____.

If I could choose a talent I don't have right now, it would
be _____.

The big difference between what you see on the outside
and what's going on inside me is _____
_____.

The one personal question that would most embarrass
me is _____.

SPILL YOUR GUTS!

When you learn the truth about me, you will understand that I am _____.

HOW I SEE YOU

In this section, all the statements are about
how the **RESPONDENT** sees the **READER**,
(the person reading the statements).

1. When you look at me, you see _____.

2. The thing you like most about me is

_____.

3. The thing you dislike most about me is

_____.

4. My most prominent body feature is my _____.

5. The one thing about me you don't know is

_____.

6. If I have a dark side, it's probably _____.

7. If you could change anything about me it would be _____.

8. When others look at me, they see _____.

9. The one thing about me that attracts people is _____.

10. One thing about me that I'm not aware of is _____.

11. If I were an animal, I'd be a _____.

12. If I were a color, I'd be _____.

13. The one word that comes to mind when you think of me is _____.

SPILL YOUR GUTS!

14. One thing you know about me that I'm not aware you know is _____.

15. When it's my turn to answer questions, I'll probably _____.

16. If I'm living a lie, it's probably _____.

17. If you were me, the biggest risk you'd take right now is _____.

18. When you hear my name, the feeling you have is _____.

19. The biggest fear you have playing this game with me is _____.

20. The funniest thing about me is _____.

21. A thought or feeling you've had about me but never expressed is _____.

SPILL YOUR GUTS!

A LITTLE BIT OF EVERYTHING

 22. When Satan whispers in my ear, he says,

" _____."

23. The one thing about men that women don't understand is _____.

24. The one thing about women that men don't understand is _____.

 25. My first command to my magic genie would be to turn me into a _____.

26. If I had to spend the rest of my life as a character in a famous book, it would be _____.

27. If I could perform miracles, my first would be

_____.

28. The best thing human beings can do for themselves is _____.

29. If there were no such thing as money, I'd be working at _____.

30. The biggest undeveloped talent I have is

_____.

31. A book I read that really impressed me was

_____.

32. The greatest kindness ever shown to me was

_____.

33. If I could get a line in the history books, it would say, "_____."

SPILL YOUR GUTS!

34. The wildest thing I ever saw while driving my car was _____.

35. The wildest thing I ever did while driving my car was _____.

36. One thing about the Bible I don't understand is

_____.

37. If I were to pick up the phone right now and, out of the blue, call someone I haven't talked to in years it would be _____.

38. The most difficult emotion for me to express is

_____.

39. If I were to begin a business right now, it would be

_____.

40. When I think of myself as very old, I see a vision of _____.

41. The wisest thing I ever did with money was _____.

42. The way I get in touch with nature is to _____.

43. The most fun I have by myself is _____.

44. The worst neighbors are the ones who _____.

45. Being around _____ makes me nervous.

46. The New Year's Eve I'll never forget was _____.

47. My fondest Christmas memory is

_____.

48. Parents are best when they _____.

49. The one virtue I admire in others that I need to develop in myself is _____.

50. The one aspect of my life that comes closest to being perfect is _____.

51. The height of politeness is _____.

52. To this day I'm still curious about

_____.

53. The highest praise you can give a person is

_____.

54. Human beings have made the most progress in

_____.

55. The most courageous act I've ever witnessed was

_____.

56. If I lost everything and didn't have a penny to my name, the very first positive act I would take is

_____.

57. The easiest way to start a conversation with a stranger is to _____.

58. If I hosted a radio talk show, I'd always be talking about _____.

59. The most fun I ever had in the rain was

_____.

60. If I had to spend the rest of my life selling something, it would be _____.

61. The greatest inspiration you can give another person is _____.

62. The first movie I produce will be the story of

_____.

63. The best thing modern science has done for humanity is _____.

64. The best question you can ask a person to find out who they really are is " _____?"

65. On airplanes, why do people always

_____?

66. The most interesting thing about my mother's relatives is _____.

67. The most interesting thing about my father's relatives is _____.

68. If I were to laugh at the funniest thing I do, I'd be laughing at _____.

69. The thing that bugs me most about supermarkets is _____.

70. The very best thing you can teach a person to do is _____.

71. I would love to star in a television commercial for _____.

72. The eleventh commandment should be _____.

73. If everyone told the truth, there would be _____.

74. Time began when _____.

75. If heaven exists it probably looks like

_____.

76. One character in literature I really admire is

_____.

77. The one thing most people do that I just can't tolerate is _____.

78. If I were to teach people one skill I've learned, it would be how to _____.

79. Why do people in checkout lines always

_____?

80. One piece of wisdom I've read that I've committed to memory is _____.

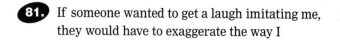

81. If someone wanted to get a laugh imitating me, they would have to exaggerate the way I

_____.

82. The most exciting time in history was

_____.

83. Honesty may be the best policy, but it can get you into a lot of trouble when _____.

84. The most soothing word in our language is

_____.

85. Most successful marriages are built on

_____.

86. If I had to live on an island for the rest of my life, I'd pick the island of _____.

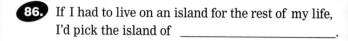

20 SPILL YOUR GUTS!

87. Aside from a belief in a supreme being, the one thing all religions have in common is

_____.

88. I simply must congratulate myself on

_____.

89. If I had lived in the Old West, I probably would have been a _____.

90. I'd rather die than be caught wearing a _____.

91. The most useless job in the universe is

_____.

92. My favorite knock-knock joke is

_____.

93. When I am very old, I will probably be the kind of senior citizen who _____.

94. The kindest person I know is _____.

95. Aside from reading and writing, every human being should be required to learn how to
_____.

96. The laughter I remember most happened when
_____.

97. In a former life I was a _____.

98. The most beautiful name I ever heard was
_____.

99. The first thing I notice when I look in the mirror is my _____.

100. Television is at its best when
_____.

SPILL YOUR GUTS!

101. When all is said and done, the greatest joy in life is _____.

102. I have great compassion for _____.

103. The biggest problem I have with organized religion is _____.

104. The most beautiful building I ever saw was _____.

105. For worldwide peace to happen, we all must first _____.

106. The type of motorist who drives me bonkers is _____.

107. I love old people who _____.

108. The biggest phony of all current public figures is

_____.

109. Why do pregnant women always want to

_____?

110. If I could imagine myself at my own funeral, I would see _____.

111. The greatest influence on people's thinking today is _____.

112. If all the events of the twentieth century were to flash before my eyes, the one picture that would stand out for me is _____.

113. The biggest reason we have been unable to eliminate wars from the human condition is

_____.

114. The most dramatic event in my family's history was _____.

115. The one battle I love to fight is _____.

116. Today I learned _____.

117. The biggest change I've witnessed in society is _____.

118. Young people today have no idea what _____.

119. The worst food served over the counter is _____.

120. Why is it every time a cop pulls you over, he or she _____?

121. The wackiest thing that ever happened to me on an airplane was _____.

122. If I had to spend the rest of my life in the most fun environment in the world, it would be

_____.

123. My feelings are always telling me to

_____.

124. The most talented person I've ever met was

_____.

125. The greatest game in the world is _____.

126. The biggest surprise I ever received in my life was

_____.

127. If I were the only person left on earth, I would find my joy in _____.

128. The most difficult decision to make in life is

_____.

129. My favorite monster is _____.

130. If I could have changed the course of one event in history it would have been _____.

131. Of all the technological advances I've seen, the one that excites me most is

_____.

132. The biggest joke God plays on the human race is

_____.

133. I think the root of all evil is _____.

134. The one myth I enjoy keeping alive in my life is

_____.

135. The most important ritual I perform every day is

_____.

136. Of all the guided tours I've taken, the one I will never forget is _____.

137. The one word that best describes my life is

_____.

138. If people are born to do or be one thing then I was born to _____.

139. The most intriguing idea I've heard in some time is

_____.

140. The toughest deadline I'm working under right now is _____.

141. I helped turn a life around when

_____.

POLITICS AND
CURRENT EVENTS

142. The biggest threat to democracy is

_____.

143. If there is a World War III, it will probably start in

_____.

144. The educational system isn't working because

_____.

145. One way the government could support families is

_____.

146. You can eliminate graffiti by _____.

147. When I think of the future of our country, I see

_____.

148. The first woman president will be _____.

149. The death penalty should be _____.

150. To be an American today means

_____.

151. The greatest advantage to exploring outer space is

_____.

152. The policy for gays in the military should be

_____.

153. To be a conservative means _____.

154. To be a liberal means _____.

155. Ending domestic violence should start with

_____.

156. Talk radio is _____.

157. Affirmative action should be _____.

158. The United Nations is _____.

159. The greatest living statesman we have is

_____.

160. Allowing women in the military to fight in combat is _____.

161. The most effective way to reconstitute the American family is _____.

162. The person most unlikely to run for president but best suited to lead the country is _____.

163. The best way to have gun control is _____.

164. If big business took over the government bureaucracy, the most noticeable difference would be _____.

165. The one aspect of our foreign policy that makes me mad is _____.

166. Anyone who burns the American flag in protest should be _____.

167. The Confederate flag still flying over some government buildings in the South should be

_____.

168. Cloning human beings should be _____.

169. President John F. Kennedy was assassinated by _____.

170. The Vietnam War proved that _____.

171. The crudest behavior threatening public civility is _____.

172. Rap music is _____.

173. The real issue between black America and white America is _____.

174. History books should be rewritten to show that _____.

175. The shocking events of September 11, 2001, changed the way I think about _____.

176. We have so much crime because _____.

177. The criminal trial jury found O. J. Simpson not guilty because _____.

178. If I ran for public office, my main issue would be _____.

179. Allowing people of the same gender to legally marry will probably result in _____.

180. My most radical political view is _____.

181. Prayer in the schools should _____.

182. The war on poverty should start with

_____.

183. If this country were to lose its leadership role in the world, it would be because

_____.

184. The deep-down reason racism exists is because

_____.

185. The one law that should be repealed is _____.

186. The most aggressive remedy to the drug problem would be to _____.

187. The best way to teach young people the value of personal responsibility is _____.

188. The central question in the abortion issue is

_____.

189. Whether a person has the right to take his or her life should depend on _____.

190. Pornography should be defined as _____.

191. The increase in teenage suicides is because

_____.

192. Distributing condoms in school sex-education courses will lead to _____.

193. If the trend toward one-parent families continues, the biggest effect on society will be

_____.

194. Putting TV cameras in the courtrooms produces

_____.

195. The most dangerous person in the world today is

_____.

SPILL YOUR GUTS!

196. Assuming the World Wide Web continues to expand, the biggest effect on politics will be

_____.

197. If the United States were to drop all immigration quotas, the biggest change to our way of life would be _____.

 198. Bilingual education should be _____.

199. The best way to reestablish people's belief in our political system is to _____.

 200. When all is said and done, more women in the workforce will produce _____.

201. The biggest myth of democracy is

_____.

MY OPINION ON EVERYTHING ELSE

202. Greatest invention: _____.

203. Smartest animal: _____.

204. Most important thing you can do:

_____.

205. God is: _____.

206. Best song ever written: _____.

SPILL YOUR GUTS!

207. Worst catastrophe: _____.

208. Most attractive body part of the opposite sex:

_____.

209. Funniest TV show: _____.

210. Most powerful word in the English language:

_____.

211. Most sinister word in the English language:

_____.

212. The greatest time waster: _____.

213. Worst ongoing pollution: _____.

214. The biggest lie: _____.

215. Success is: _____.

216. Most overrated person in history: _____.

217. Funniest clown: _____.

218. The information superhighway will lead to:

_____.

219. Christmas means: _____.

220. UFOs are: _____.

221. The Devil is: _____.

222. Heaven is: _____.

223. Most exciting motion picture: _____.

SPILL YOUR GUTS!

224. Real loneliness is: _____.

225. Most shocking accepted behavior:

_____.

226. Most ignorant thing people do:

_____.

227. The thrill of a lifetime: _____.

228. Most peaceful thing you can do: _____.

229. Religion is: _____.

230. Marriage is: _____.

231. Ghosts are: _____.

232. The most valuable skill: _____.

233. Greatest act of kindness: _____.

234. Most hypocritical person alive: _____.

235. Most important thought in the world:

_____.

236. The reason we're here: _____.

SPILL YOUR GUTS!

MAN VS.
WOMAN
ZONE

IT'S A MAN THING

 237. The difference between how a man thinks about sex and how a woman thinks about it is

_____.

 238. Men see their car as _____.

 239. The reason little boys are more aggressive than little girls is _____.

 240. Men look upon conflict as _____.

 241. Sexual harassment exists because

_____.

242. When a man uses the word *bitch,* he means

_____.

243. The big difference between a man's sense of humor and a woman's is _____.

244. The biggest change in men's behavior as a result of the women's movement has been

_____.

245. Power for a man means _____.

246. Men like their lovers to wear trashy clothes in the bedroom because _____

_____.

247. The reason males generally score higher than females on mathematics tests is

_____.

248. The feminist movement is generally viewed by men as _____.

249. Men define masculine as _____.

250. The most common reason men cheat on their wives is _____.

251. Aggressive females turn many men off because _____.

252. Intimacy for a man means _____.

253. Men admire women who _____.

254. Men can't stand it when women _____.

255. Most men are suckers for a woman who _____.

256. A man's greatest fear in marriage is

_____.

257. Men who date older women do so because

_____.

258. Men who date younger women do so because

_____.

259. Men usually don't communicate all their emotions
because _____.

260. The reason men fall asleep right after sex is

_____.

261. The biggest threat modern women pose to men is

_____.

262. A man's biggest misconception about marriage is

_____.

SPILL YOUR GUTS!

263. Happiness to a man means _____.

 264. Men feel most free when _____.

 265. In business, a man's greatest natural asset is

_____.

 266. As much as a man may try to conduct a successful relationship, I don't think men will ever learn how to _____.

 267. When the joy of sex leaves a relationship, a man's first impulse is _____.

 268. Of all the qualities that make men and women compatible, the one thing that makes them most incompatible is _____.

 269. The easiest way to a man's heart is

_____.

270. If men could have babies, they would

_____.

271. Most men are fascinated by large breasts because

_____.

272. The biggest mistake most men make on the first date is _____.

273. Sexual prowess to a man means _____.

274. To a man, "showing his feminine side" means

_____.

275. Men were created to _____.

276. The design flaw in a man's nature is

_____.

277. The easiest way to deflate the male ego is

_____.

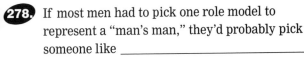 **278.** If most men had to pick one role model to represent a "man's man," they'd probably pick someone like _____.

 279. The one trait of traditional masculinity that seems to be disappearing is _____.

 280. The real reason most men are awkward when buying lingerie for their significant other is

_____.

 281. In the future, the most dramatic change in the male role in relationships will be

_____.

IT'S A WOMAN THING

 282. Women want men to be more _____.

 283. The big difference between flirting and sexual harassment is _____.

 284. Romance means _____.

 285. Women hate it when a man _____.

 286. Women love it when a man _____.

 287. Working at a relationship means _____.

288. An unmarried female's greatest source of pride is usually _____.

 289. Women need _____ more than men.

 290. The nicest compliment you can give a woman is _____.

 291. A woman's most effective asset in conflict is her _____.

 292. The strongest natural ability a woman has as a businessperson is _____.

293. The difference between how men compete in sports and how women compete is

_____.

294. The biggest advantage a woman would bring to the office of president of the United States would be _____ 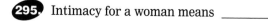.

295. Intimacy for a woman means _____.

296. Women are more sensitive about their _____ than men are.

297. Female drivers have a tendency to

_____.

298. A woman's greatest personal fear is that

_____.

299. The best way to win an argument with a woman is to appeal to her _____.

300. The most hurtful criticism you can level at a woman is _____.

SPILL YOUR GUTS!

301. Women outlive men because _____.

302. A female's ego is based on _____.

303. The one thing about the mother–daughter relationship that most men don't understand is

_____.

304. The best way to keep a woman interested in lovemaking is _____.

305. A woman sees greatness as _____.

306. The one male habit that most annoys women is

_____.

307. The easiest way to deflate a woman's ego is

_____.

308. One thing more than any other that strengthens a woman's self-esteem is _____.

309. If most women had to pick a role model who represented a "woman's woman," it would probably be _____.

310. If most women had to pick a role model who represented a "man's man" it would probably be

_____.

311. Women feel most free when _____.

312. A woman's greatest misconception about marriage is _____.

313. Women's daydreams are usually about _____.

314. The biggest reason women like to shop is

_____.

SPILL YOUR GUTS!

315. The one trait of traditional femininity that seems to be disappearing is _____.

 316. When women say they want more communications from their men, they really mean _____.

 317. The biggest mistake most women make on the first date is _____.

 318. Sexual prowess to a woman means _____.

 319. To a woman, "showing her masculine side" means _____.

 320. Women were created to _____.

 321. The greatest self-doubt that most women have about being a mother is _____.

322. In the future, the most dramatic change in the female role in relationships will be

_____.

 323. When the joy of sex leaves a relationship, a woman's first impulse is _____.

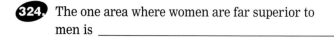 **324.** The one area where women are far superior to men is _____.

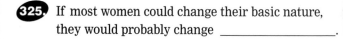 **325.** If most women could change their basic nature, they would probably change _____.

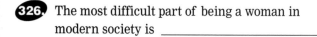 **326.** The most difficult part of being a woman in modern society is _____.

IT ALL STARTED WAY BACK WHEN...

327. The very first thing I remember as a child is

_____.

328. The one word that best describes my childhood is

_____.

329. My funniest memory is _____.

330. The most interesting person from my childhood
was _____.

331. The biggest fear I had when I was small was _____.

332. As a child, I was most proud of _____.

333. The funniest name I remember is _____.

334. My hero was _____.

335. When I was alone, I used to _____.

336. My favorite toy was _____.

337. I found out about sex when _____.

338. The naughtiest thing I did was _____.

339. When I daydreamed, I had visions of

_____.

340. I thought I was really good at _____.

341. My biggest secret was _____.

342. I had a crush on _____.

343. I never understood _____.

344. I first learned about death when _____.

345. The one smell that still lingers in my memory from those days is _____.

346. The biggest monster in my life was _____.

347. I wanted to be _____ when I grew up.

348. In school I had the hardest time learning

_____.

349. My favorite game was _____.

350. When I played "make-believe," it was always about

_____.

351. When I was punished, it was usually about

_____.

352. The day I cried the hardest was _____.

353. I couldn't stop laughing when _____.

354. The moment I felt most loved and most secure was

_____.

355. I think I knew my childhood was over when

_____.

356. The one thing I always wanted but never received
was _____.

357. When I picture my neighborhood, I see

_____.

358. I loved it when my mom and I would

_____.

359. I loved it when my dad and I would

_____.

360. My most prized possession was _____.

361. My happiest day was _____.

362. If I could talk to the little kid that used to be me, I'd say, " _____."

363. No one ever answered me when I asked

_____.

364. Once, when no one was looking, I

_____.

365. I used to do a funny imitation of

_____.

366. When I heard God's name mentioned, I had an image of _____.

367. I always felt safe when _____.

368. A word I remember from those days is

_____.

369. My secret hiding place was _____.

370. The silly joke I told all the time was

_____.

371. I'd give anything if I could be a kid again and once more experience _____.

THE FIVE MOST DANGEROUS UNFINISHED PERSONAL STATEMENTS

372. If I became my evil twin, I would immediately _____.

373. If I were to "lose it all" and have a complete mental breakdown, it would probably happen because _____.

374. The revenge I secretly seek is to _____.

375. The guilt I carry around with me is _____.

376. The one part of my sexuality that is out of control is _____.

ON THE EDGE

377. The day I didn't think I'd make it was
_____.

378. I almost got caught when _____.

379. When things get rough, the one consoling
thought I have is _____.

380. I'm most afraid when _____.

381. The biggest risk I could take in my life right
now is _____.

382. My recurring nightmare is _____.

383. My most consistent self-destructive behavior is _____.

384. The most dangerous person in my life is

_____.

385. The most dangerous thought I have is

_____.

386. The most dangerous thing about me is

_____.

387. The mistake I keep making that could land me in big trouble is _____.

388. If I don't change _____ my health will suffer.

389. The ultimate danger for any human being is

_____.

SPILL YOUR GUTS!

390. I fought like a tiger when _____.

391. The odds were against me when _____.

392. I've got to learn to say no to _____.

393. The day my behavior was most reckless was _____.

394. I would describe my temper as _____.

395. The one area of money management I am most inept at is _____.

396. I am very sensitive to people criticizing my _____.

397. I should have listened to my intuition when _____.

398. People give me lots of space when I start

_____.

399. The easiest way to take advantage of me is to

_____.

400. You get on my bad side when you

_____.

SPILL YOUR GUTS!

THE DEEP-DOWN ME

401. The biggest "why" question in my life is: Why is _____?

402. I live by the slogan _____.

403. The first impression I give people is

_____.

404. I am moved to tears when _____.

405. The one authority I respect more than any other is _____.

406. If I had the power to make the world better, the first thing I'd do would be to

_____.

407. The one thing I need to let go of is

_____.

408. Children teach me that _____.

409. The most persistent message I get from my inner voice is _____.

410. I still have a deep burning desire to

_____.

411. If my mother were describing me, she'd say

_____.

SPILL YOUR GUTS!

412. If my father were describing me, he'd say
_____.

413. The biggest excuse I make for not doing the things that are really important to me is
_____.

414. My greatest sense of appreciation is for
_____.

415. The closest I've ever come to suicide was
_____.

416. When I hear the word *home,* I think of
_____.

417. The most consistent criticism people make of me is _____.

418. The thing people like most about me is

_____.

419. If I had the guts to chuck it all and pursue my dream, I'd _____.

420. The most daring thing I ever did was

_____.

421. The one thing that always makes me laugh is

_____.

422. My self-esteem is highest when _____.

423. The one human being in the world I admire most is _____.

424. I wish I were really good at _____.

SPILL YOUR GUTS!

425. My most obvious inherited characteristic from my father's side of the family is my

_____;

from my mother's side, it's my

_____.

426. The best investment I ever made in another human being was _____.

427. Of all the mysteries in the world, the one that confounds me the most is _____.

428. Of all the mysteries in the world, the one that confounds me the least is _____.

429. I have a natural talent for _____.

430. The type of personality that drives me up the wall is _____.

431. I lose my temper when _____.

432. The one thing about me that I fear the most is _____.

433. If there is a God and I could ask Him any three questions, the first would be

_____?

The second would be

_____?

The third would be

_____?

434. The best way to describe me as a friend is

_____.

SPILL YOUR GUTS!

435. The one thing that brings me back down to earth when I am on my high horse is

_____.

436. The most consistent lie I tell is

_____.

437. I am most ashamed of _____.

438. The funniest thing about me is _____.

439. If I had to boil my life down to one central message, it would be _____.

440. The one word I am most fond of is _____.

441. All I really need to be happy is

_____.

442. The biggest misconception people have of me is _____.

443. If you are what you eat then I am _____.

444. The most difficult event I've had to deal with in my life was _____.

445. My "Plan B" in life is _____.

446. When I need fun and laughter in my life I _____.

447. The one thing that always calms me down and makes me immediately aware of what is most important in life is _____.

448. I have always been most optimistic about _____.

SPILL YOUR GUTS!

If you asked my friends what my greatest ability is, they would say _____.

450. The number one thing you need to know to get along with me is _____.

451. Other than my family, the one thing in the world I would die for would be _____.

452. The one common thread in all the stories of my life is _____.

453. The one event that had the most influence on my life is _____.

454. Of all the movies I've seen, the one I identify with the most is _____.

455. What I like most about me is _____.

THE SECRET ME

456. The best description of the dark side of my nature is _____.

457. The most surprising thing about me that people don't know is _____.

458. When I'm alone, I sometimes _____.

459. The weirdest thing I ever tried was _____.

460. If I were to put a costume on the "secret me," it would be a _____.

461. The biggest accident I ever caused was _____.

SPILL YOUR GUTS!

462. I may never forgive _____.

463. One of the strangest thoughts I ever had was _____.

464. When I talk to myself, the conversation is usually about _____.

465. Something I've done that nobody knows about is _____.

466. The one material thing I want that I know I'll never get is _____.

467. My pet name for myself is _____.

468. The one person I should call and say "I'm sorry" to is _____.

469. I sometimes sit for a long time and look at a photograph of _____.

470. The time I was most untrue to myself was _____.

471. The closest I've come to living a fairy tale was _____.

472. Sometimes a voice inside says to me,
"_____."

473. If I were to get wild and funky in my retirement years, I'd probably start _____.

474. The advice people give me that I should take but don't is _____.

475. When I look in the mirror I think _____.

SPILL YOUR GUTS!

476. The agreement I once broke was _____.

477. If I had to forgive myself for something, it would be _____.

478. An alibi I frequently use is _____.

479. I've made a secret pact with myself to _____.

480. If you really want to rattle my cage, ask me _____.

481. The one person I should call and say "I love you" to is _____.

482. A grudge I've been carrying around for a long time is _____.

483. An evil thought that keeps popping up in my head is _____.

484. When I pretend to be or act like somebody I'm not, it's usually because _____.

485. When I picture my own death, I usually see

_____.

SPILL YOUR GUTS!

FANTASY

486. The greatest pickup line I ever heard was,

"_____."

487. The sexiest thing I do is _____.

488. My most consistent fantasy is _____.

489. A perfect romantic evening for me is _____.

490. To be a better lover I have to _____.

491. The one thing that turns me on more than any other thing is _____.

492. If I were starring in a porno film, I'd be

_____.

493. My favorite sex game is _____.

494. The one word that describes my lovemaking is

_____.

495. My most embarrassing moment in lovemaking
was _____.

496. The most daring sex act for me is

_____.

497. The funniest thing about sex is

_____.

498. The word that turns me on most is _____.

499. My perfect mate would have to have

_____.

500. The scariest encounter I had with sex was

_____.

501. I have a secret desire to _____.

502. The ideal honeymoon would be _____.

503. If I enrolled in Sex College, the first course I would take would be _____.

504. My most disastrous date was _____.

505. I like to be kissed on the _____.

506. The sexiest thing I ever saw at work was

_____.

507. I once stumbled in on _____.

508. When I arranged to act out a fantasy, it was all about _____.

509. The sexiest gift I ever gave was _____.

510. A love relationship without lust is _____.

511. The one-night stand I remember most vividly happened when _____.

512. My first experience with sex was _____.

513. The best way to keep passion alive in a relationship is to _____.

514. If I were going out on a first date and I wanted to show that person exactly who I am, I would
_____.

 515. The best way to satisfy a man is
_____.

 516. The best way to satisfy a woman is
_____.

517. If I opened the door and saw a person of the opposite sex standing there naked, the first thing I would say is, "_____."

518. I pick up the phone and call Dr. Ruth. My opening line is, "Dr. Ruth, please help me. I'm having trouble with _____."

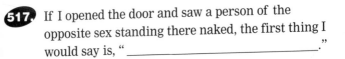 **519.** If I had to put a tattoo on a private part of my body, I would put a tattoo of _____ on my _____.

520. The biggest lie I ever told a person of the opposite sex about myself was _____.

 521. Seduction works best when _____.

 522. The most unusual place I ever had a romantic encounter was _____.

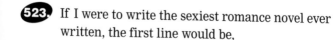 **523.** If I were to write the sexiest romance novel ever written, the first line would be,

"_____."

 524. The sexiest outfit a person of the opposite sex can wear is _____.

525. Usually, the first thing about me the opposite sex sees and likes is _____.

LIARS' BLANKS

526. If I were to take all my clothes off right now, you'd see a very large _____ on my _____.

527. I know I've got someone in the palm of my hand when I _____.

528. When I feel romantic, I have a tendency to _____.

529. People always say I look a lot like _____.

530. I once registered in the general election to run for the office of _____.

531. While cruising on a luxury liner, I once

_____.

532. In high school I won the title of

_____.

533. Years ago, I was caught wearing _____.

534. If you were to go through my personal effects at home, the one item that would mystify you is

_____.

535. When I don't get my way, I very often

_____.

536. I had a very small part in the movie

_____.

537. The wildest piece of clothing I have in my closet is

_____.

SPILL YOUR GUTS!

538. I was blown away when I met _____.

 539. When I can't get to sleep, I sometimes get up and start _____.

 540. My biggest brush with the law was _____.

 541. The most unusual pet I ever had was a _____.

 542. In a school play I once had the role of _____.

 543. The biggest shock I ever gave my mother was _____.

 544. People couldn't stop applauding when I _____.

545. One day when I just felt I wanted to be bad, I went out and _____.

 546. Once, in the middle of a date, I shocked the other person when I _____.

 547. I am most proud of a trophy given to me by

_____.

 548. As far as I know, I still hold the record for

_____.

 549. The craziest thing I ever heard that happened on a honeymoon is _____.

 550. The one bona fide criminal I had personal contact with was _____.

 551. I came very close to making the evening news when _____.

552. When I kiss, I have a habit of

_____.

553. I once astonished a large group of people when I

_____.

554. I felt the hand of God when _____.

555. The most famous person I ever spoke to was

_____.

FREE ASSOCIATION

Quickly speak the word or words that jump into your mind when you hear the following terms.

556. Fear / _____.

557. Government / _____.

558. Worry / _____.

559. Exotic / _____.

560. Sin / _____.

561. Fame / _____.

562. Achievement / _____.

563. Fun / _____.

564. Summer / _____.

565. Death / _____.

566. God / _____.

567. Laughter / _____.

568. Leader / _____.

569. Regret / _____.

570. Nostalgia / _____.

571. Erotic / _____.

572. Destiny / _____.

573. Soldier / _____.

574. Independence / _____.

575. Spooky / _____.

576. Mother / _____.

577. Future / _____.

578. Opportunity / _____.

579. Loneliness / _____.

580. Fascination / _____.

581. Father / _____.

582. Sensitive / _____.

583. Hollywood / _____.

584. Me / _____.

585. If / _____.

586. Cheating / _____.

587. Envy / _____.

588. Heaven / _____.

589. Outrageous / _____.

590. Manipulate / _____.

591. Saturday morning / _____.

592. Santa Claus / _____.

593. Graduation day / _____.

594. First place / _____.

595. True love / _____.

596. Summer vacation / _____.

597. Impossible job / _____.

598. Scared stiff / _____.

599. Wildest party / _____.

600. Almost there / _____.

601. Foolish pursuit / _____.

602. Special gift / _____.

603. Bad habit / _____.

604. Biggest improvement / _____.

605. Constant yearning / _____.

HOLLYWOOD

606. Sexiest actress of all time: _____.

607. Sexiest actor of all time: _____.

608. Motion picture that had the greatest impact on society: _____.

609. Best musical: _____.

610. Biggest scandal: _____.

611. The king of tear-jerking movies: _____.

612. Funniest motion picture: _____.

613. The most evil villain: _____.

614. Most memorable scene: _____.

615. The line I'll never forget:
  "_____."

616. Saddest motion picture: _____.

617. The one character I'll never forget:
  _____.

618. The movie that came closest to my life:
  _____.

619. The worst movie of all time: _____.

620. The role I would have loved to play: _____.

621. A movie I never understood: _____.

622. I cry every time I see _____.

623. The scene that gives me the creeps is

_____.

624. A movie song I'll never forget: "_____."

625. I would have rewritten the ending to

_____.

626. Why haven't they made a movie about

_____.

627. The one movie I never wanted to end was

_____.

628. One actor or actress who never fails to fascinate me is _____.

629. The film I most closely identify with my youth is _____.

630. The most overrated actor or actress in Hollywood today is _____.

631. The best action-adventure movie of all time is _____.

632. If you want to put your date in the mood for romance, you should rent the movie _____.

633. The next technological jump in moviemaking will be _____.

634. The movie that probably set new fashion trends was _____.

635. The best movie monster of all time was

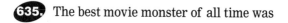

.

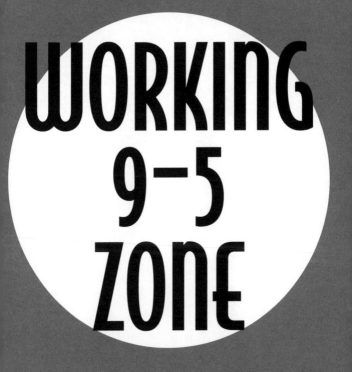

TAKE THIS JOB AND . . .

636. The most important skill a manager should have is _____.

637. My job gives me _____.

638. The thing that bothers me most about my work is _____.

639. The biggest advantage I have over other people I work with is _____.

640. Building an effective team starts with _____.

641. The kind of people I work with that bug me the most are the people who _____.

642. I get the most satisfaction on my job when _____.

 643. The biggest danger in the American workforce today is _____.

 644. When I hear the term multicultural workforce, the first thing that comes to my mind is _____.

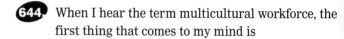 **645.** The easiest way to get people to do more is _____.

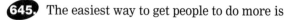 **646.** The most effective way to motivate a work team is _____.

 647. My all-time dream job would be _____.

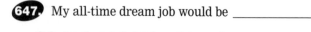

648. The most fun I ever had at work was

_____.

649. The best communications skill is _____.

650. Joy at work comes only when _____.

651. If there is a best way to get along with the greatest amount of people most of the time it is

_____.

652. My current success plan is _____.

653. If I had to add a skill that would push me to the next level of achievement, it would be

_____.

654. The best customer service I ever received was

_____.

655. The worst customer service I ever received was

_____.

656. The most effective time-management technique is

_____.

657. The thing that gets most people in trouble at work
is _____.

658. I think sexual harassment is _____.

659. The silliest thing I ever saw on the job was

_____.

660. I usually handle stress by _____.

661. The day I was most inspired was _____.

662. If I were to write a book on how to be successful at work, its title would be _____.

 663. If I could look my boss in the eye and say anything I wanted, I would say,
"_____."

 664. Excellence means _____.

 665. If I were put in charge of a brand-new team, the first thing I would tell the people on it is
_____.

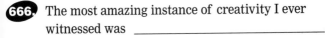 **666.** The most amazing instance of creativity I ever witnessed was _____.

 667. My boss doesn't understand that _____.

 668. The only meetings that work are _____.

669. The best piece of criticism I ever received was

_____.

670. The best-kept secret of being a winner at work is

_____.

671. If everybody who works with and for me were surveyed, they would say I was _____.

672. I get recognized and praised for specific actions when I _____.

673. My philosophy of being a good boss can be summed up by saying, "_____."

674. I positively can't stand _____.

675. The last new thing I learned to do was

_____.

676. If I were going to produce an outrageous comedy skit about some process at work, it would be

_____.

 677. The most effective interview question you can ask a job applicant is _____.

 678. If I were asked to create a whole new way of getting my work done, it would be

_____.

 679. The greatest leader I ever met had the ability to

_____.

 680. The most negative thing I do to myself that holds me back is _____.

 681. I felt most appreciated when _____.

682. For me to be the success I want to be, I have to learn to _____.

683. The biggest rumor making the rounds is

_____.

684. If one of the scandal-sheet magazines exposed something at my work site, the headline would read, "_____."

685. When I'm long gone from my present job and my name is mentioned, the first thing people will say is, "_____."

LET YOUR IMAGINATION FLY

 686. The first thing Adam said to Eve was,

"_____."

687. Two babies walk into a bar. One bangs his fist on the bar and says, "_____."

688. Mrs. Patrick Henry said, "Give me liberty or give me _____."

 689. I look into your eyes and suddenly I feel

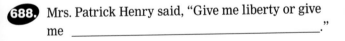

_____.

690. The one-word title of my new opera is _____.

691. Never eat anything that _____.

692. The *Mona Lisa* has that smile on her face because _____.

693. I was born to _____.

694. A good rule to follow is: When in doubt, _____.

695. When I am very old, I will wear _____.

696. A wise man once said that the real difference between men and women is _____.

697. I often wonder if Superman has a _____.

SPILL YOUR GUTS!

698. 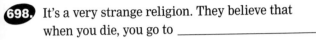 It's a very strange religion. They believe that when you die, you go to _____.

699. I have this awful nightmare that a giant paper clip is trying to _____.

700. 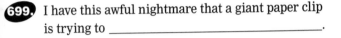 The best thing to do with belly-button lint is

_____.

701. A strange inner voice is always telling me to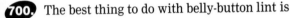

_____.

702. I knew it would be a bad day when I woke up and saw a _____.

703. 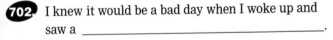 I walked into the spa and people seemed shocked when they looked at my _____.

704. Elvis came to me in a dream and said,

" _____."

705. It's a little-known fact that Beavis and Butthead are _____.

706. My first assignment as a government spy was to _____.

707. George Washington's real name was _____.

708. I once put a whole _____ in my mouth.

709. It was obvious I was starting my midlife crisis when _____.

710. My gangster name is _____.

711. If I were a voyeur, I'd probably be watching _____ all day.

712. I'd like to have a secret meeting with _____.

713. I heard they invented a computer that

_____.

714. The title of my new hit CD is *Love Is Nothing More Than* _____."

715. CNN interviewed me about _____.

716. Our food supply ran out and we were forced to eat

_____.

717. My creation of the world's most bizarre pizza is called _____.

718. If I had to spend the rest of my life as an organ of the body, I'd be a _____.

719. The funky nudist camp required all members to

_____.

720. It was an unusual group-therapy session where everybody was required to _____.

721. I've learned that the worst thing you can do on a first date is _____.

722. I'm told I'm the only person in the world with a Ph.D. in _____.

723. There I was at thirty thousand feet, coming out of the clouds, when suddenly _____.

724. I walked to the center of the stage, looked a hundred thousand people in the eye, and

_____.

725. The title of my new extravaganza show in Las Vegas is _____.

726. I've just been appointed dean of _____.

727. The battle cry of my revolution is "Down with _____."

728. I get uncontrollably romantic whenever I hear _____.

729. A wise old man with a long, flowing white beard once told me that the secret to a happy life is to always _____.

730. I never fail to stun an audience into silence whenever I _____.

731. I am the only player in football history who ever _____.

732. I am preparing a secret life as a

_____.

733. The original Shakespearean line was "To be or not

_____."

 734. The most fun I ever had in a nudist camp was
playing _____.

735. There's a new genetically engineered body part
that allows human beings to

_____.

 736. If I could talk to anybody in history, I would speak
to _____ and ask this question:
"_____
_____?"

737. The first line in my autobiography would be
"_____
_____."

738. If I were captured by space aliens, this is how it would happen: _____.

739. The world started when _____.

 740. If I could be anybody else in the world, I'd be _____.

741. The person in the world most like me is _____.

 742. I win big money in the lottery. The first three things I do are _____

and _____

and _____.

743. If I had the power to organize a reunion of any group of people in the world, living or dead, it would be a reunion of _____.

744. I would love to hear the private confessions of _____.

745. In a previous life I was a _____.

746. The luckiest moment in my life happened when _____.

747. If I were going to invent something, it would be _____.

748. The most fun you can have on planet Earth is _____.

749. If I had the guts, the wildest practical joke I would like to play is _____.

750. Sex on Mars is entirely different from sex on earth. Up there they _____.

751. If I were a psychiatrist, my specialty would be _____.

752. The ultimate hero would be somebody who _____.

753. If I could get a standing ovation from an audience for anything I do, I'd want that recognition for _____.

754. My friends say the most outrageous thing about me is _____.

755. If I were to be at the center of a national scandal, it would be _____.

756. If I were to become an extremist at any one of my present behaviors, it would probably be

_____.

757. The craziest relative in my family is/was

_____.

758. If I had to spend the rest of my life in a line of work devoted to helping others, it would be

_____.

759. When I die and face my Maker, the first question He will ask me is, "_____?"

760. If they were to produce a soap opera based on the story of my life, the steamy title would be

_____.

761. The animal I am most like is a _____.

762. If I were to create a new sensation in fashion, it would be _____.

763. When I take on another persona, I pretend I am

_____.

764. The end of the world will come when

_____.

765. If I had a severe inferiority complex it would probably be because I have a _____.

766. The last words I will speak are "_____."

767. If I were a great historic villain, I would be

_____.

768. Aside from my family, the one person in the world I would most want to spend eternity with would be _____.

769. If I were a great historic hero, I would be

_____.

770. My ultimate T-shirt would have these words on it:

_____.

771. The first sentence in my eulogy should be,
"_____."

772. If I were being interviewed for an exposé magazine, the most provocative question they could ask would be, "_____?"

773. The one list book I would write is *1001 Ways to*

_____.

774. Plastic surgery would do me the most good on my

_____.

775. If I could take one thing away from human nature it would be _____.

776. When I become old and eccentric, the one thing I will do that will tick off the most people is _____.

777. If I could bring to the afterlife the one possession that meant the most to me, it would be _____.

778. I've always wanted to make an obscene phone call to _____.

779. The one newspaper headline I'm dying to see is, " _____."

780. If I could eliminate one person from the universe, it would be _____.

781. The one extravagance I'd love to have in my life is

_____.

782. If I could be God for twenty-four hours, I'd

_____.

783. The one period in history I would have most liked to live was _____.

784. I'd love to call in to work sick with a weird excuse like, "_____."

785. If I came face-to-face with the Devil, my first words would be, "_____."

786. I'd like to have the private phone number of

_____.

787. When I look into my crystal ball, I see that the future will be filled with _____.

788. My personalized license plate reads _____.

789. Suddenly, I become invisible. The first place I go is _____.

790. My two-word epitaph is, " _____."

791. If I could relive one moment in my life, it would be _____.

792. If I were to get a sex change, the one reason would be _____.

793. The closest supernatural experience I've had was _____.

794. The height of luxury for me would be to _____.

795. Give me the power to bring back from the dead one person in history and I'd bring back

_____.

 796. My life as a cartoon would be called,
"_____."

 797. If I had to judge whether or not mankind should continue based on my lifetime experiences, my judgment would be _____.

798. The spookiest story I ever heard was

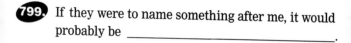 _____.

799. If they were to name something after me, it would probably be _____.

 800. If I decide to become an eccentric artist, I'll probably concentrate on _____.

801. The weirdest thing you would find in my closet is
_____.

802. If I could pick a heroic way to die it would be
_____.

803. I'd like to open the most unusual fast-food chain in the world, devoted to _____.

804. My command performance at the White House would be _____.

805. My first question to the pope would be,
" _____?"

806. If I had a circus act it would be _____.

807. I'd love to be the spokesperson for _____.

808. My next reincarnation will be as a _____.

809. I'm forming my own cult based on the belief that

_____.

810. My personal ad in the classified section reads:
"Desperately seeking _____."

FUTURE
ZONE

CREATING A BETTER WAY

 811. I would end homelessness by _____.

812. If I were going to design a new article of clothing for men, it would be _____.

813. If I were going to create a new article of clothing for women, it would be _____.

814. The way to end all traffic jams is
_____.

815. A whole new way of running a presidential campaign would be to _____.

816. If I could change human nature, I would make sure that _____.

817. A more realistic form of marriage would be _____.

818. The one course that should be taught in all primary and secondary schools is _____.

819. The best way to raise an intelligent child is _____.

820. If I were to reform the judicial system, I would start by _____.

821. To keep our political leaders more in touch with what the people are thinking, we ought to _____.

822. If I were to produce the most original radio talk show in the world, it would be

_____.

823. I am designing an educational system that ensures that every citizen is given all the life skills necessary to achieve success. The most basic course covers how to

_____.

 824. The most effective neighborhood-watch crime-prevention program would be one where

_____.

825. I've been asked to give a speech to a local high school on the danger of drugs. I start off with the most dramatic demonstration ever seen in this program. It is _____.

 826. If I gave my worst fear a silly name, it would be

_____.

827. I've invented the most amazing pill in the universe. When people take it they

_____.

828. A new safety device for automobiles would be

_____.

829. The most truly heroic act I could perform in my life right now would be to _____.

830. In my concept of a perfect world, all negative people would have to _____.

831. A unique way to reform juvenile delinquents is

_____.

832. The most productive way to use the capabilities of retired persons is _____.

SPILL YOUR GUTS!

833. A totally different way to present the evening news would be to _____.

834. If I were to open up the most important school in the world, it would be a school devoted to teaching _____.

835. The best way to alleviate passengers' fears that their baggage has not been loaded onto their flight is _____.

836. If I were to design the most unusual shopping mall in the world, it would be one where _____.

837. The name of the new self-help book I am writing for children is _____.

838. I've opened an amusement park called Real Life. The most popular ride is _____.

839. A foolproof way to teach people how to perform extraordinary customer service is

_____.

840. The name of my new superhero for modern times is _____.

841. If I were to change everything about me, the biggest difference would be _____.

842. The most significant thing I could do to further the cause of world peace would be to

_____.

SPILL YOUR GUTS!

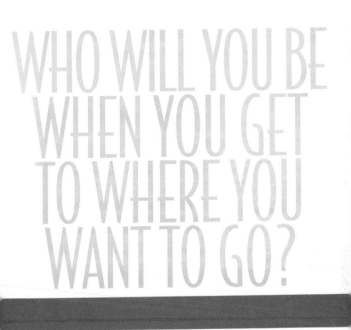

WHO WILL YOU BE
WHEN YOU GET
TO WHERE YOU
WANT TO GO?

843. Your biggest dream was to become

_____.

844. After you achieved that, the most significant thing you did with your success was

_____.

845. The greatest obstacle you had to overcome was

_____.

846. The most fun you had being successful was

_____.

847. Of all the lessons you learned getting to the top, the most important one was

_____.

848. Once you achieved everything you wanted, you turned around and started helping others by

_____.

849. The greatest legacy you leave your family will be

_____.

850. Your experience has taught you that real success is _____.

851. All the material success in the world is meaningless unless you have

_____.

852. The one word that destroys more people than any other is _____.

853. The biggest chip you carried around on your shoulder was _____.

854. Your biggest toy was _____.

855. You almost lost it all when _____.

856. If you had never been born, the biggest loss to this universe would have been

_____.

857. The one person, other than yourself, most profoundly affected by your success was _____.

CRYSTAL BALL

858. War will be _____.

859. Marriage will be _____.

860. Families will be _____.

861. Personal computers will be _____.

862. Education will be _____.

863. Jails and prisons will be _____.

864. Soldiers will be _____.

865. Movies will be _____.

866. Music will be _____.

867. The greatest discovery will be _____.

868. The _____ will be the most powerful people on earth.

869. Everyone in the world will be able to

_____.

870. The answer to the biggest mystery in the universe will be _____.

871. Automobiles will be _____.

872. The most popular pill in the world will be one that

_____.

SPILL YOUR GUTS!

873. The biggest danger will be

_____.

874. The most sought-after product will be

_____.

875. The highest-paying job will be _____.

876. The most sensational amusement park ride will be

_____.

877. Science will develop a nasal spray that will

_____.

878. Automobile accidents will be avoided by a device
that _____.

879. Stand-up comedians will make the most fun of

_____.

880. The biggest nostalgia craze will be

_____.

881. The most popular collector's item will be

_____.

882. It will be very fashionable to _____.

883. The biggest debate will be _____.

884. Dying will be _____.

885. It will be mandatory that all human beings

_____.

886. The most watched TV show will be

_____.

887. The most valuable personal skill will be _____.

888. Work will be _____.

889. The hottest profession will be _____.

890. The best way to make money at home will be _____.

891. Paradise will be discovered to be _____.

892. _____ will be out of control.

893. The number one tourist attraction will be _____.

894. Heroes will be people who _____.

895. The biggest lie exposed will be _____.

896. The most devastating conflict will be between _____ and _____.

897. As I lie dying, I will be able to say that the one thing I did to make this world a bit better was

_____.

SPILL YOUR GUTS!